bloom

E M Salisbury

BookLeaf
Publishing

India | USA | UK

Presentation by *BookLeaf Publishing*

Web: www.bookleafpub.com

E-mail: info@bookleafpub.com

ISBN: 978-93-5761-185-5

First edition 2022

DEDICATION

This is dedicated to the mother of my mother. Nana Rena. Your soft sweet soul lives on in me and my words.

ACKNOWLEDGEMENT

Thanks to my wee mammy, Jane. You taught me to love with an open heart, and dream with a wild imagination. To my brother Dean. You showed me how to escape the sore and nippy grasp of life through games and movies. To my soul's friends. Coco, Liam, Naomi, Rach, Suz, Iris, Aimie, Denika - you always believed in me. I am forever in awe, and in debt to your support. I love you all. And finally, to my husband. You are my muse. You are my starry night. You are the fabric of my universe. Bless you. Thank you, thank you, thank you.

PREFACE

This is for the poor kids with rich dreams. Don't
sell yourself short.

Salt

I tried to make an ocean out of you
Wild and free
Rushing and pushing
Crashing and pulling
I tried to fill you with all this wild life
I tried to make you calm, smooth and strong
But your wave came and washed over me
Sending back to shore with nothing but your
salt.

abba

If you asked me what music I like, I would say
"I like a bit of everything!".

If you asked me about the TV shows I've been
watching, my reply would probably be "Oh, you
know, little of this, little of that!".

But after 26 years, scuffing my shoes on the
pavements of this earth
I want to shout:
I fucking love disco. Nothing makes me more
happy than a bit of disco.
Nothing makes me feel more human than
listening to soft folk pop music.

I'm so malleable
I bend and reshape myself to be more
comfortable
To be more neutral
Safe zone for anyone
No strong opinions
I've been on the fence so many times, for so
long
That the skelves in my skin are turning gangrene

Decomposing beliefs
Rotting my decisions away
I don't know who I am.
I can spout my name and age like it means
anything. But when it comes down to what
makes me who I am inside.

My mouth dries up like the sun is setting on the
horizon of my tongue.
I don't know who I am because I have made and
remade myself so many times.

Who do I want to be this week? Who's haircut
will I replicate? Who's outfit styles can I copy?
Who's catch phrase can I plagiarise today?

I wish I felt unique, but I feel recycled. I long to
feel organic, but I'm simply a greenhouse made
of plastic bottles.

I can be filled with flowers and tomatoes, but I'll
never be glass.
I mould myself to a new shape like play-doh,
just in the hopes people will like me.

And although I may be ready for people to like
me for who I am, I can't do that because I don't
know who that is.

Spent so many years malleable, I forgot my
material.
My superpower is shape-shifting.
But I wish I could fly.

You can ask me
A hundred questions
And my answer will be
I don't know
My favourite music to be still to
An artist I relate to
A sport I'm good at
But I don't know

I don't know how to begin
In telling you
What makes me who I am
I only have those three words
As an automatic reply
I don't know

I know I am a daughter
A wife and a sister
I know I am a friend
You can count on to listen
But as for what makes me unique
I don't know

For tomorrow I could feel

Like autumnal colours are my thing
The next I could stay in bed
The day after that
I could wear the baggiest top
In nothing but black

I am not the moon

Dear Father,
I am not the moon
Though I am a celestial being of sorts
My veins run red with cosmic matter
And my hair shines almost as bright as the sun

I am not the moon
Though my face has small craters
My skin always sports a soft shade of grey
And my tears are tranquil seas

I am not the moon
Nor is the moon me

The ways I love may be out of this world
But I am not the moon
My freckles may be sequenced like skies full of
stars
But I am not the moon
My love cannot wax, nor wane
For we are not the same

Lunar has phases
My bisexuality does not

Cairngorm

Flowers grow
Under the fence
Under the handrail
Right by the door
Mint green paint
Sleeps on these walls
Echoed by voices
Of when you would call
But I'm glad
You've gone
Because this place
Is more of a empty house
Than a loving home now

therapy

I want to be the reason my eyes dilate
I want to make my own heart race
Compliment myself and administer the butterfly
belly feeling for myself
I want to look at myself and heard birds singing
I want to dress myself in silk
And take it all off for myself
Be raw for myself
Open and honest to myself
I want to be the reason I get up in the morning
and fell asleep with a smile
I want to whisk myself away on romantic trips
And have dinner by a softly lit river
I want to hold myself
Tell me its okay to hurt
Rub my own back
Play with my own hair
I want to fall in love with me

Tommy and Rena

A thorn took shelter in the bottom of my foot
As I was playing beside the blossom tree
I cried at its unannounced arrival
So sudden
You appeared like a shadow on a wall
Soft and expected
And tweezered the thorn out
A kiss on the head was my reward
You held me
As my face became moist with emotion
You called it another Saturday morning
I call it
The memories of your garden

Purgatory

I'm not sure if I believe in an afterlife
That's not to say I don't want to believe
The idea of everlasting paradise with passed on
loved ones is heavenly
But I don't know what to expect
Does it all shut off when the light in our eyes are
gone?
Like awaking from a dreamless sleep
You remember nothing except
It was nighttime outside the window when you
closed your eyes?
I want to believe
Because I have so many questions
They rattle around in my brain when the sun has
finished her shift
Like a tombola drum
Significant in their own way but chosen at
random from my incessant 2am thoughts while I
am staring
into the darkness of my eyelids
If I cannot have answers or justice when living
as a physical form
I stay hopeful that as a spirit I will know the
answers

Ambition

I want to live a million lives
The trombone player in a soft jazz band looking
over the skyscraper landscapes at sunset
He fanatic frog person charging her way through
the busy jungle with rain on her forehead
I wanna be the apartment artist living in paint
splattered dungarees and watering her plans
The crochet girl slumping around in a Cardigan
making crochet tote bags at christmas
I want to be it all
Every woman under the stars
Every lifestyle and passion and love for the earth
But the reality is a grey bleak wash
A blur of nothing
A cloud of indecisiveness and lack of motivation

OCD/ADHD

On goods nights,
My mind is like the circus
The smell of cotton candy
The excitement and joy in the air
The sound of fun being had
Music you haven't heard in ages
Blissfully echoing in the background
It's like imaginative socialising
Maybe that person is there
The one who I've been meaning
To get coffee with
Maybe they have a nice scarf on
And maybe we share a laugh
Over some silly memory
It's buzzing with life
It's noisy but in a comfortable way
On bad days
It's like walking home
In a rainstorm
In the dark
At 3am
Noisy aggressive drunks slurring and shouting
Wanting to run but not wanting to be seen
As someone who is scared

It's loud and overwhelming
The smell of sick
The dread and longing to get home safe
The sounds of bottles smashing into the tarmac
Voices yelling insults you've had hurled at you
before
Bringing back old conversations
Questioning responses
Wondering if I'm the voice
Who yells the insult
In other people's bad day brain
It's just
Invasive fright
It's like hell
Some days when the circus is in town
I wonder if
Even the circus lights are too bright for me
If the rotation of the carousel
Is why I'm falling over
Nitpicking
At what could be ignorant bliss

Antisocial

I'm in the mood to socialise
When nobody is interested
Like a lonely little bird whistling for a friend
Into an empty forest
"I'm ready to socialise now, don't you want to
go out and have fun?"
But they're all out
In their flocks
And I'm sitting alone again
Perched on this cold fucking branch
Wondering why I'm like this
Why couldn't I have been born fucking normal

Dissociative

I spoke words to you today
My voice like a background buzz
My throat mimicking television static
Fuzzy screen behind my eyes
Recordings rolling out of my molars
Falling into an unlistening space
You were tuned to a different channel
Updated and fresh
A different perspective being reported

Sensory Overload

The tick of the clock
Feels like a tiny hammer
Fracturing the spaces
Between my ears
And so
With each second
Irritation boils
Like a pot of water
So close to bubbling over the rim
I breathe
For the facade of happy
Is the golden ticket to social acceptance
Without it
I'm scared I will never
Be in contest
To be
Crowned a winner

2am

I stare into space
In the soft blueish glow
From the refrigerator
A gentle draught
Lifting the hairs on my arms
Standing like thin soldiers
Stationary blonde
My eyes watering staring
Staring
Staring
Worlds and imagery
Swirl around my brain
Stirring together like soup
On the brink of boiling

dangerously in love

I wilt
In the arms of you
Bent over and flopped
My neck on the edge of your wrist
I writhe at your touch
It feels poisoned
Every tip of your finger
An arrow doused
With the supple black juice
Of the deadly nightshade
Which arises from the soil
Outside my window
Now,
My bones burning
A red hot pulsing glow
Inside this flesh foundation
I call my home
Alarm bells violently ring
Echoing in every dark corner
Of my foggy mind
My gut screaming
"Get out!"
My heart screaming
"How?"

stormy weather

You are like a storm
I can always tell
When you're on your way
As the skies get darker
And the air around changes
And every hair
On my arms
Standing to attention

wife

A cold white moon still in the sky
Casting shadows under it's power
My head pressed on a pillow
Like a plaster for a wound I have not yet needed
I think of you
How you make me feel like a watering can,
Spreading life and splashing kind everywhere I
go
I picture you in a forest of greens and shadows
A painter's dream because you are full of beauty
I could sit you in any garden and you would
always be the wildest flower to me
Your petal blooming fuchsia
Of kind words and little things you do for me
Your gorgeous stem slender and strong
Like the spine that holds you
Your inner pollen holder
A scent so sweet the bees are magnetized to
dance to your location
A scent so sweet I could use you in tea
Your leaves so delicate
Just like the look in your eyes when I apologise
Your roots so pure and untangled and well
watered

Never having known the knots of mental doubt
Never known the worms that slither around you
I think to myself of how I can help you grow and
blossom further
I am your watering can, feeding you and
nourishing you like the sun and her rays
beaming down
Giving us wild life and freckled skin
Burning us with her scolding anger
Kissing us on early morning rises
I can't wait to one day plant seeds with you in
the garden of our life.
My soil fresh and prepared and water at the
ready to rain down some life on us

overthinkin

Why can't I sleep?
Is something on my mind?
Maybe a secret I can't keep?
I see the sky change
The night time blue to the morning range
I stare at the ceiling
Strobes form above me
As cars outside light up their journey
The silence is deafening
I am so used to my busy head
That the lack of sound
Pours into me
Filling me with existential dread
I can't wait to dream
Technicolor fantasies
Wild stories
But none of them
Can be told
If my eyes don't close

concrete and tar

One of my favourite things of the Earth
Is seeing the cracks in pavements Flourished
with weeds
No matter how hard the concrete may be
Nature wins unendingly
Nature finds the hidden passage by herself
Like the secret villain room behind the book
shelf
She pulls on the pavement
A wiggle through unfazed by cement
She bursts through broken brick
Her green growing quick
All to reach the sun
And I think its so beautiful
Man made substances don't stand a chance
When Mother Nature is given a task
I try to take something from that Maybe I can
rise and burst and reach far
Even when suffocated in concrete and tar

Eavesdropping

I think the plants in our home
Continue to grow so well
Because they eavesdrop
On all the kind and beautiful words
You dress me in

love at midnight

We were eating cheesecake
That we made with our bare hands
At half past midnight
You sipped from your cold cows milk carton
And I sipped from my cold oat milk carton
I looked into your eyes
Is this heaven?
We kiss with milky moustaches
And stood still as our bellies soft and full with
happiness
"Bedtime?" You say,
With a large hand gently cupping my elbow
Like a sculpter holding their masterpiece
"Yes, my love. Bedtime."

But who needs sleep
When every moment of you
Is nothing short of dreamy

music

I'm listening to
Comptine d'un autre été
And every note feels like a memory
Familiar in it's melancholic haunt
The rhythmic pattern of each stroke
Reminding me of passing days
When the wind, wintery and cold
Would chill my nose and the tips of my ears
It feels like vintage silk
It feels like black and white movies
Where the voices
Are loud
Dramatic
Emotional

www.ingramcontent.com/pod-product-compliance
Lightning Source LLC
LaVergne TN
LVHW021336200726
843509LV00014B/2552